CHRISTIAN ENGAGEMENT IN POLITICS

EDMUND S. P. JONES

THE SAINT ANDREW PRESS

EDINBURGH

CHRISTIAN ENGAGEMENT IN POLITICS

First published in 1975 by
THE SAINT ANDREW PRESS
121 George Street, Edinburgh

© Edmund S. P. Jones 1975

ISBN 0 7152 0328 2

Printed in Great Britain by
Howie & Seath Ltd.
Duncan Street, Edinburgh

CONTENTS

HOW TO GET INVOLVED: *In International Affairs*

HOW TO GET INVOLVED: *In Local Affairs*

THE PARTY SYSTEM

APPENDIX: *For Your Consideration*

****

PREFACE

Many contemporary Christians who sing about 'a green hill far away' frequently forget that Jesus of Nazareth was executed about 9 a.m. on that fateful Friday morning on the grounds that he posed a threat to the political stability of the area. Crucifixion was the normal Roman punishment for crimes against the State and Jesus of Nazareth died as a political criminal. In His short ministry He had said that a caring relationship for one's neighbour, especially the poor, the hungry, the destitute, and the despised, was an integral part of serving God. To care about how people are treated is politics.

But Christians have not always found it easy to relate this faith, with its concern for others, to the complex apparatus of the modern state. And sometimes the attempt to do so has led to highly unattractive results. Yet the issue cannot be shirked. The Gospel may be given among the pitch-pine pews on a Sunday morning, but it is clearly given _for_ the redemption of the world. How can Christians who are concerned both for the church and for society, for faith and for freedom, for the Magnificat and for the Manifesto, fulfil their discipleship? This booklet is offered as a simple guide to those who want to think seriously about some of the problems raised and subsequently to act with courage, knowledge and humility in witness to their Lord.

I am most grateful to Mrs. Catherine Buchanan for her careful typing of the manuscript and to my publisher, Mr. Tim Honeyman of The Saint Andrew Press, whose encouragement and professional skill have done so much to bring the project to a successful conclusion.

THE SCENE IS SET

A TRUE STORY

On the morning of 17th June, 1816, the portly Bishop of Ely
entered his cathedral for a special service. He was preceded by
his butler carrying the sword of state in token of his civil
jurisdiction, and accompanied by the Chief Justice of the Isle to
whom he had just given breakfast. The choir sang three anthems.
A sermon was preached on 1 Timothy, 1:9 "The law is not made for
a righteous man, but for the lawless and disobedient". The
service ended with the Hallelujah Chorus. From there the Chief
Justice proceeded to the court-house and tried 75 men who had
rioted in the conditions of near famine and unemployment which
followed the Napoleonic wars. Twenty-three men and one woman
were convicted. Five were hanged. Nine were transported to a
penal colony. The remainder were given prison sentences.

The Bishop himself had bills of 25s. for hangman's ropes,
5 guineas for a cart and two horses for the condemned men, and
13s. for a chaise for a clergyman to accompany the criminals to
the gallows. A group of fenmen swore over the coffins that they
would tell generations yet unborn what the bishops and gentry had
done to their kin.

ANOTHER TRUE STORY

On 28th March, 1968, a Baptist minister led a protest march through
the streets of Memphis, Tennessee. The marchers were protesting
against the conditions in which the black garbage workers had to
do their menial and dirty job. The garbage collectors had no job
security and no insurance. The leather tubs in which they hauled
the refuse on their shoulders were old and leaky, causing painful
blisters. The men were not allowed to eat lunch in the cafes. No
washing or toilet facilities were provided. When they sought
shelter on porches from the torrential rains for which Memphis is
noted the enraged white owners called the police. On 1st February,
1968, two crew members took refuge from a torrential downpour in
the barrel of their garbage lorry. It was a huge cylinder with a
powerful steel mechanism that compressed the garbage into tightly
packed bales. By accident a shovel was dislodged, short-circuiting
the machinery. The men made frantic efforts to escape but were
unable to climb out. They were crushed to death. There was no
workmen's compensation, no benefits for family or children.

The black workers went on strike, but Mayor Henry Loeb III, a
proud opinionated man, refused even to discuss grievances. So a
massive protest march was organised to publicize conditions and
secure redress. It was led by a Baptist minister. His name was
Martin Luther King.

AND A THIRD ...

In February, 1906, a twin boy and girl were born into the home of
a German consulting physician and university lecturer. The boy,
who was named Dietrich, was one of eight children who were brought
up in that happy and well-to-do home.

During the First World War when death stood at the door of
almost every home the family moved to Berlin. And it was there
that Dietrich Bonhoeffer grew up. During a year's work in Spain
as an assistant minister he collected examples of children's games
which reflected the old disputes between Christian and Moslem. He
even tried his hand at bull-fighting.

In the Germany of the early thirties most Christians supported
Hitler. It seemed that the only valid alternative to Nazism was
Bolshevism. Indeed Hitler spoke often of completing the work of
Luther. He talked of Jesus as the hero of all right-minded people.
He tried to end party squabbles within the church. He encouraged
his brown-shirted Hitler Youth to go to church. Bonhoeffer openly
criticised Hitler's interference in church affairs and his attack
on the Jews.

In 1942 he met the Bishop of Chichester in Sweden with secret
proposals for a negotiated peace which would involve the arrest of
Hitler and the establishment of an alternative government on
honourable terms.

He was arrested in April 1943 and spent the next two years as
a political prisoner in Nazi concentration camps. Through corres-
pondence, much of it in code, Bonhoeffer kept in touch with the
resistance movement and the church. On 8th April, 1945, he was
executed by a firing squad at Flossenburgh.

THE CHOICES

Each story illustrates a way in which the church has tried to play
its part in the political life of society.

In the first, the church maintained a close liaison with the
civil authorities in the governing of society. Frequently Bishop
and Baron virtually controlled the life of the community between
them.

In the second, a Baptist pastor became deeply involved in the
social problems of his race without jettisoning the work of
evangelism and pastoral care.

In the third, a churchman felt called upon to join the under-
ground resistance movement to seek the overthrow of the elected
government of the day.

Each was different from the other. But they shared the belief
that Christians must be involved in the total life of a community,
not least those areas of civic life where the issues are controversial, the means questionable, and compromise unavoidable.
For them politics was a legitimate concern of the Christian.
Were they right?

ARGUMENTS AGAINST CHRISTIAN INVOLVEMENT IN POLITICS

(a) The Church is a religious organisation. Its job is to cater
solely for the inner spiritual life of men. Its goal should be
spiritual regeneration, not social rehabilitation.

(b) Politics is a dirty business. If the church becomes
involved in areas where expediency and frustration are unavoidable the purity of the gospel will be compromised. Political
preferences can seldom claim moral sanctions.

(c) Christ specifically avoided a political role. He showed
little interest in changing institutions, whether they were
ecclesiastical or imperial or civic. He was solely concerned
with individuals - a leper here, a blind man there.

(d) The prime job of the church is to act as a <u>reconciler</u> between
men of different classes, races, nations and parties. It cannot
do this if it takes sides. Furthermore it is virtually impossible
for the church to speak with one voice on a controversial issue
since its own members will be divided.

(e) History provides too many examples of how the church which
has sought power has ended up by compromising love. Where the
church has achieved temporal power it has frequently used it for
the benefit of itself rather than the enrichment of mankind. It
is hard to think of a single instance where ecclesiastical
domination of politics has not been incompetent, platitudinous,
or tyrannous.

ARGUMENTS FOR CHRISTIAN INVOLVEMENT IN POLITICS

(a) Christians start from the fact that "God so loved the <u>world</u>
that He gave His only begotten Son". So the gospel is about the
whole of life, not just the private concerns of the individual
or the domestic life of the church.

(b) The Bible never suggests that Christians have no obligations
to the world. On the contrary it directly links doing justly and
caring for one's neighbour with doing the will of God. We cannot
care for our neighbours without being drawn into practical politics.

(c) It is absurd for Christians to act as though the gospel had

nothing whatever to say about the Russian Revolution, the rise of
Hitler, the "final solution" of the Jewish problem, the end of
colonialism, the destruction of Hiroshima, and the painful birth
of social justice in large tracts of the globe. The prophets
spoke of God as the agent of the social and political change which
was constantly going on around them.

(d) The stewardship of power is as important as the stewardship of
money. Educating the masses, providing security for the aged and
infirm, protecting the weak, and caring for the inadequate is a
Christian responsibility which in the end is directly affected by
political decisions.

(e) The church is involved in politics already: e.g. Bishops of
the Church of England and members of the Church of Scotland who
are peers in their own right may sit in the Upper House. In many
townships there is the annual Kirkin' of the Council and public
prayers are offered on set occasions. The issue is how ordinary
Christians can more effectively exercise their ministry in the
civic and political life of the community.

(f) Politics may be a dirty business but a church which is
primarily concerned with keeping its hands clean will end up
having no hands at all. The reason why some young people turn to
organisations like 'Shelter' and 'Oxfam' rather than the Christian
Church is not so much that they have doubts about God, or distaste
for religious services, but that they feel the church no longer
offers genuine and costly leadership in the struggle with evil.
In most local congregations by far the greater part of time,
money, energy, and organisation is devoted to the internal
interests of the church rather than to serious involvement with
the problems of society. A glance at the Sunday Intimations will
confirm how domestic are most of the concerns of church members.

A MIDDLE WAY BETWEEN THE EXTREMES

Pressed to its logical conclusion the first set of arguments
implies a total separation between Christianity and politics.
The church would become an exclusive sect made up of those un-
tainted by the traffic and sordidness of the world.

On the other hand enthusiasts of the second line of reason-
ing have seemed sometimes to believe that the church should
infiltrate the world, convert its institutions, and create the
Kingdom of God in society.

Perhaps the truth lies somewhere in between. But the
middle ground is not always easy to discover. In theory it
would be agreed that the church should be a prophetic minority
(Acts 5: 29ff), and maybe act as the conscience of the nation
(Acts 2: 37). In practice it is not always easy to see how this
works out. Does the Bible give any clear guidance on the problem?

THE BIBLE SAYS

THE OLD TESTAMENT

A NATION IS BORN

When an ancient Israelite spoke of his faith he started with God
not as Creator, but as Liberator of people. The story had been
told over and over again around the camp-fires at night when the
Hebrews were nomads, in the market-places when the Jews became
city dwellers, and in the synagogue schools where children learned
to read and write. Story telling revealed the meaning of the
Jewish faith without committing the error of trying to define it.
This was the story.

A Prince of the Egyptian Court, called Moses, watched day by
day as Jewish slaves were forced to build vast towns for the
Pharaoh in the Nile Delta. Their gang-drivers were as merciless
as the eastern sun which burned down pitilessly on the wretched
backs of the slaves. And Moses was angry. For an inner voice
told him that this was a blasphemy which cried to heaven. He was
determined by God's help to put it right.

But approaches to the authorities produced little effect.
Only after ten separate attempts did Moses even manage to get a
verbal assurance that the conditions of the slaves would be
improved. In the end he led a walk out. It climaxed in a mass
escape from the labour camps of Egypt and the gradual forging
together of a new people who had a vision of a land flowing with
milk and honey where all men would live in peace and justice.

THE LIVING GOD

This experience was the beginning of all the Hebrews came to believe
about God, their role in the world, and the purpose of living.
Moses became to the Jews what the Pilgrim Fathers became to the
Americans and Lenin to the Russians, and Mao Tse-tung to the
Chinese. From that day forward their God was the One who had set
them free from serfdom and called them to be his people.

He was not primarily a God like those of other peoples whose
deities were associated with the natural phenomena of earthquakes
thunder and fertility. He was the living God who cared about
whether people were free, and living as brothers in just and com-
passionate dealings with each other. This was what the Old
Testament writers meant when they spoke of the righteousness of
God. "For what doth the Lord require of thee but to do justly,
to love mercy, and to walk humbly with thy God."

THE IMPORTANCE OF THE LITTLE MAN

The problem of politics is that too often the rulers forget they
are dealing with people. The party becomes more important. The
individual is there to be manipulated, cajoled, bribed, exploited,
or forgotten according to the needs of the system, the policy, or
the manifesto.

So the Old Testament shows us courageous men who were not
afraid to speak in the name of the Lord against those who wielded
economic and political power for their own advancement without
respect for the rights of the little man.

When King David authorised the liquidation of Uriah in a
suicide mission so as to get his wife, Nathan the prophet chal-
lenged him in the name of the Lord. (2 Sam. 11-12)

When Jezebel arranged for perjury and a miscarriage of
justice so that Ahab could appropriate Naboth's small-holding
Elijah stepped in to the arena. (1 Kings 21)

When Micah found that the judges were crooked (Micah 3: 9-12),
Jeremiah saw that the landed gentry were paying starvation wages
(Jer. 22: 13-16), Amos discovered that judicial palms were being
quietly greased (Amos 5: 12) and Isaiah realised that those who
were not able to contribute to the Gross National Product (Isa. 1:
13-17) were forgotten by those in power they did not hesitate to
speak out. "He judged the cause of the poor and needy ..... Is
not this to know me? says the Lord." (Jer. 22: 16)

THE QUALITY OF LIFE

It was not only the prophets who were concerned at the quality of
civic life and the integrity of those who held economic and
political power. The Law included legislation for the welfare of
the deaf and blind, the treatment of slaves, the rights of the
poor, and the place of the immigrant. (Lev. 19: 10, 14, 33-4;
Deut. 15: 11-15)

Similarly each of the last five commandments was originally
designed to secure one of the fundamental rights of the individual.
The sixth safeguarded his life, the seventh his marriage, the
eighth his freedom, the ninth his reputation and the tenth his
property.

The real battle in the Old Testament between the prophets of
Yahweh [1] and the devotees of pagan deities was not over the number
of gods. Rather the central question concerned the nature of the
true God and the role of his followers.

1 *(See next page)*

6

For Moses and those who accepted the Sinai tradition Yahweh
was the living Spirit active in the contemporary movements of
social change. He was the One who acts. He was the God of
history. And because this was His nature to follow Him meant to
be involved in the events that affected men and nations. To opt
out was to be disobedient.

In contrast the pagan deities like the Baalim of the
Canaanite tribes were identified with the rhythm of nature. In
them men were not the initiators of new events but spectators in
the annual cycle of nature. The present and the future lay wholly
in the lap of the gods and man had no responsibility for initiat-
ing change or controlling events.

---

1 *YAHWEH* - The origin and precise meaning of this designation is
unclear. The point is that in Ancient Near Eastern society to
name someone is to know the character of that person. If YHWH
means 'He causes to be' or 'He will be' then a free translation
of God's answer to Moses (Ex. 3: 13-15) would be: "I am the God
who is active in whatever circumstances you are called to face,
the God whose character is promise and fulfilment".

THE NEW TESTAMENT

THE MAN WHO CAME

Palestine is a comparatively small country, about 150 miles long
and 75 miles broad. It is smaller than Switzerland and about half
the size of Scotland. Jesus Himself never set foot outside an
area twice the size of Inverness-shire. His life and death were
scarcely noticed in the ancient world. It was asking a lot of
people to expect them to believe that a joiner's lad born to a
Jewish teenager in the late Roman Empire could have anything
earth-shaking to say to the world.

Here was a youth who lacked any professional status, an
itinerant Rabbi who had never been to an Academy of any distinction, a preacher who failed to convert the crowds, a leader who
only had three followers faithful to the end - and they were
women. What possible threat could He have been to Imperial Rome?

But a Jew of the first century could no more be disinterested
in politics than an Englishman of the nineteenth century could be
neutral towards the monarchy. Judaea was an intensely political
and troublesome corner of the Empire.

From the time of the fateful Maccabean rebellion some 160
years earlier governmental life had been marked by a series of
bitter power struggles between the various factions.

THE PARTY LABELS

There were the Herodians who hoped for a restoration of the Kingdom
of Herod the Great. Herod's family and descendants were hated by
the people as half-breeds and puppet Kings. The lasting impression
that Herod's insane cruelty made upon the people is preserved in
the story of the Innocents Massacre (Matt. 2: 13-18).

There were the Zealots who sought to win freedom from the
occupying forces by terror and assassination. For them the only
good Roman was a dead Roman. At least one member of the organisation was one of the twelve disciples.

The Sadducees were an hereditary aristocracy of about two
hundred families who controlled the Temple and with it the treasury.
In return for collaborating with the Romans in preserving the
status quo they provided the people with the illusion of self-
government.

Furthermore Jesus used politically explosive terms such as
'Kingdom' and 'Messiah' to explain His message. In the end the
Man from Nazareth was executed on a political charge. Around the
time of his final entry into Jerusalem there seems to have been a

8

bloody uprising by a band of patriots led by Barabbas (Mark 15: 7).
Maybe it even sparked it off.

Seen against this background it is surprising that Jesus had
so little to say about the political situation. Indeed there is
only one place in the gospels where the power of the state is
explicitly mentioned (Mark 12: 13 ff), though Jesus is aware of
crimes against humanity especially those which affect His own
people (Luke 13: 1 f). But political problems always take second
place. Explicit statements on major social and political issues
of the day such as totalitarian government, reprisals against
civilian populations, slavery, and the limits of taxation are
notable only by their absence. Why was this? Was Jesus uninteres-
ted in the immediate life of His community though it was marked
by an evident lack of political freedom, oppressive taxation, and
an ever lengthening list of martyrs? It is easy to overtax the few
incidents in which Jesus does say something about a political issue
and to try to draw out more implications than they contain.

The omission is probably due to the belief in the imminence
of the End and the dawn of the Kingdom. The reign of God is about
to be ushered in.

THE KINGDOM IS NEAR YOU

Yet Jesus equally expected His disciples to make an impact in
society. They were to be the light of the world, the beacon on
the hill. Centuries-old enmities between racial and religious
groups could be changed. How? Not by force. Not by a new set of
rules. But by a new spirit. His Kingdom might not be of this
world but it would certainly be in it, often challenging and
exposing those whose political allegiances ignored the truth.

This idea of the Kingdom is the key to an understanding of
the apparent reticence of Jesus on political matters. The famous
statement about "rendering to Caesar the things that are Caesar's
and to God the things that are God's" (Luke 20: 19 f) was not meant
to suggest separate spheres of influence, or a neat dividing line
between the realm of politics and that of religion. There is not
a spiritual world where we must obey God and a secular one where
we obey Caesar. What Jesus affirmed is that the specific duty of
paying one's dues to the de facto authority responsible for civil
order does not absolve one from the total demand of God for
obedience and service. This obedience to God will have to be
renewed each day in changing circumstances, and continue long after
Empires have passed away. What Jesus was saying to his questioners
was that though the coin may belong to Caesar because he minted it,
they belong to God because He created them in His image.

In the same way the apostles showed little interest in reform-
ing the social and political order because they believed the End

was at hand. In the interim Christians should commend the gospel by being good citizens. That implied obeying the duly constituted authorities (Romans 13: 1 f) and accepting social practices of the day such as slavery (Philemon). In Acts almost invariably Christians seem to have made a favourable impact on the civic authorities (Acts 16: 38 f; 19: 24), and Paul did not hesitate to make use of the advantages which Roman citizenship conferred on him.

But he centres the work of Jesus in an idea that carries with it the most profound implications for political activity. The kernel of his teaching is that on the Cross Jesus conquered those principalities and powers which control the destinies of men and nation (Col. 2: 13-15). Just as it was the "Rulers of this age" that brought Jesus to the Cross and executed Him, so it is Jesus who defeats the powers (1 Cor. 2: 8). In an age when the party machine, the bureaucracy and the system so largely control men's lives we can glimpse the immense implications of a gospel which speaks of freedom from the powers which dominate the face of society.

JOHN SEES IT DIFFERENTLY

By the time John came to write his Revelation the state was actively persecuting the infant Church. The seer identified Caesar as "The Beast (Rev. 13: 1 f), the Anti-Christ" and a common street walker as the symbol of the Imperial Empire (Rev. 17: 1 ff). There is no common ground between church and state. There is no working relationship between the believer and the political authorities.

A CONCLUDING THOUGHT

Ultimately the main argument for the political involvement of the Christian does not depend on the interpretation of a small number of passages in the New Testament. It rests on the implication that the gospel is concerned not simply with inner conversion, but with a fundamental change in the way people relate to each other in the social life of a community.

The conflicting claims of the various political parties represent different ways of organising the relationship between man and his neighbour. Most people accept that justice, equality, freedom and self-respect are important to all communities. Political parties tend to reflect different priorities in seeking to achieve a common good. An objective like equality may require that freedom be curtailed. Peace may be achieved at the expense of justice.

The earliest group of believers quite instinctively evolved a distinctive social pattern which had similarities with the

pattern of communal life followed by the Essences, the third major
Jewish sect after the Pharisees and Sadducees. In response to
that love for one another which Christ had commanded they voluntarily sold their land and chattels to create a 'Poor Relief Fund'
(Acts 2: 45; 4: 34-35). The principle of mutual economic responsibility among believers was accepted from the beginning (Romans
12: 13; Gal. 6: 2) though the Relief Fund was increasingly
replenished out of earned income (Eph. 4: 28; cf. 2 Thess. 3: 10),
and the liquidation of all capital was soon modified (1 Cor. 16:
1-4; 2 Cor. 8: 1-15). That may seem a far cry from a church
mixed up in rates and rent-control. But the seeds of that pattern
have provided the thrust for the most important political upheavals of our day.

THE CHURCH AND ITS POLITICAL ROLES IN HISTORY

THE BEGINNING

During the governorship of Pontius Pilate Jesus of Nazareth, the self-styled Messiah and founder of a new world religion, was executed on the charge of being a political troublemaker. In the years that followed other disciples of "The Way" died as martyrs. Best known were Paul and Peter who according to rumour were put to death in Rome by the Emperor about A.D. 67.

SOCIAL AWARENESS

At first the Christian faith spread among the poor people and slaves who worked long hours, could only meet at night, and held closed meetings which were rumoured to be for immoral purposes. Though there was little sustained attempt to change the political institution of the day Christians soon began to work to relieve suffering in the world. They protested against the massacre of prisoners of war, the inhuman treatment of slaves, and the cruelty of gladiatorial contests. An important emphasis of their Faith was the conviction that basically all men are brothers because all are children of the same God. Equally important was the early distinction which Christianity made between personal conscience and the power of state. The implications of both ideas were to be far-reaching.

PERSECUTION

The political ideas of the early Christians were easily misunderstood and could lead to denunciation and persecution. The Roman Empire was ruled by the Emperor who had a status equal to that of divinity. So obeisance to Caesar was virtually synonymous with patriotism and the maintenance of the stable state. Because Christians refused to give lip-service to this way of looking at the state they were regarded as treasonable anarchists and subjected to severe persecution. But contrary to popular belief such official hostility was spasmodic with the uneasy peace reflecting the secondary importance of the church - state issue during the first three centuries. Both parties were much more concerned with their respective internal domestic conflicts. Constantine and his successors assumed that the traditional Roman civic oversight of religion should continue. It never occurred to anyone that this time-honoured practice should be abandoned just because Christianity had become the official religion of the Empire.

AUGUSTINE

St. Augustine did more than any other ancient Christian writer to
provide a viable answer to the problem of Church and state. In
his great work The City of God (c. A.D. 420) he put forward the
idea that they are really two "cities". There is the earthly and
temporal one and there is the heavenly and eternal one. The
earthly city is ordained in the providence of God to provide an
ordered framework for the maintenance of the state with due
political authority and obedience. But it has no independent
authority. It is always answerable to the spiritual power
embodied in the city of God.

So the stage was set for disputes over respective spheres of
authority, and in later times the clergy were often at logger-
heads with the civil powers.

In the end Augustine interpreted the relations of church and
state more in terms of the Old Testament kings and prophets than
in the actions of the apostles. The implication of harsh coercion led to his acceptance of force by the civil power at the
behest of the church to impose orthodoxy on dissidents and
preserve the purity of the Faith.

CONSOLIDATION AND CORRUPTION

As the Roman Empire slowly disintegrated, the Bishop of Rome
assumed a pastoral oversight of Christian work in Europe. In the
absence of a strong Roman Emperor he also took over the aura of
government and public affairs of the city. The trappings of the
Empire were transferred to the church. The Pope became the
'Pontifex Romanus'.

But what began as a pastoral duty increasingly became a
political stance. On Christmas Night in A.D. 799 the Emperor
of the West prostrated himself in obeisance before the Roman
Pope. This highly symbolical act was to continue for a thousand
years until the coronation of Napoleon in 1808 and it left a deep
impact on the church's understanding of itself. The triumph of
the Christian Faith in the world could lead to discreditable
scenes such as were fought in the name of the church as well as
its search for true spiritual and moral authority among men.
Popes like Innocent III (1198-1216) assumed full civic as well
as religious authority. At his word a King of France took a
wife, a King of England accepted an unwanted Archbishop, a King
of Leon separated from a cousin whom he had married, and a
claimant to the crown of Hungary deferred to his rival. The kings
of Bohemia, Poland, and Denmark consulted him. The monarchs of
England, Aragon, and Portugal obeyed him. The papacy was at its
zenith. For two centuries or more there was general clerical
control of secular and spiritual affairs in Western Europe. The

papacy became deeply involved in the major political objective of building a Christendom at the apex of which stood the Pope as both king and priest. But political authority was not backed by moral leadership and increasingly papal interference in secular matters was discredited.

THE REFORMATION

Luther was a scholar and a monk. But the movement of religious protest which he initiated quickly became mixed up with all kinds of political and social radicalism. Luther was shocked when the peasants of Germany, stirred up by the new religious ideas, revolted in 1524 and demanded economic and social rights, including a regulation of rents and security of tenure. Some genuine religious zeal but much more social discontent lay at the source of this uprising. Luther adamantly refused to endanger his religious reformation by linking it to social rebellion. He called the peasants "filthy swine" and urged the princes to suppress them by force. When asked by what authority the state may interfere to secure religious truth, Luther compared it to the duty of a passerby to put out a fire with all haste. Such uprisings and the need to get backing against Catholic rulers led Lutheranism into a close alliance with the state. There has been much dispute as to whether Luther saw the prince or magistrate as rightful ruler of the church by virtue of his innate civil position or whether the Christian community delegated that ecclesiastical authority to the prince as the most suitable person to exercise it. Wherever the balance lies the undoubted fact is that Lutheranism established itself under the benign protection of the civil authorities.

Calvin fell back on the old idea of two equal powers exercising separate jurisdiction but each deriving its ultimate authority from the decrees of God. Accordingly the civil magistracy is the most responsible of all human professions for in ordering public life according to scripture it fulfils God's Will for society. Accordingly full obedience to the duly ordained civil powers is mandatory and civil disobedience thoroughly abhorrent on religious as well as social grounds. On one occasion the ecclesiastical authorities in Geneva heavily penalised a citizen who had publicly criticised the arrival of French refugees on the grounds that it had increased the cost of living. The Christian citizen must obey the state implicitly. However Calvin recognised one exception to this rule. If a heretical or pagan sovereign takes steps which clearly imperil the true faith then the Christian citizen is bound to resist apostasy in obedience to God. Of course the difficulty of deciding what measures are hostile to the true faith remains. But Calvin's concern was the practical one of strengthening the hand of the Reformed princes and securing the quiet goodwill of Catholic sovereigns towards their Protestant citizens.

14

Knox was less happy with a doctrine which conceded the independent authority of the civil power. For one thing he had seen the precious work of the Reformers gravely threatened by rulers like Mary Tudor and Mary, Queen of Scots. The civil authorities, which include King and Parliament, rightfully exercise power but it must always be in obedience to the Word of God, for the maintenance of true religion and the support of the church, and in response to the will of the people.

Andrew Melville developed further the idea of the Two Kingdoms. There is the spiritual one for which the church is responsible. And there is the civil one for which the state is responsible. Neither derives its authority from the other but each receives its mandate from God. It was this sense of separate jurisdiction and spiritual independence which led to the famous occasion on which Melville told King James VI of Scotland to his face that he was 'God's sillie vassal'. The King never forgave his impunity and later confined him to the Tower. "Bishops" he said, "must rule the ministers and the King rule both."

Later Scottish history witnesses the continuing conflict between the civil and ecclesiastical authorities to secure what they considered to be their rightful sphere of influence. If James VI made exaggerated claims of civil authority even in religious matters, Melville in his more extreme moments, and often the Covenanters, went too far in the other direction. The uneasy relation between church and the state was highlighted again in the disruption of 1843. In one of the most heroic acts of church history 451 ministers out of 1203 left the General Assembly to form what became known as the United Free Church. In so doing it voluntarily surrendered sanctuary, stipend, manse and glebe rather than accept lay patronage and the attempts of outside bodies to influence the decisions and mission of the church. It was a high price to pay for freedom in the church. Ultimately Parliament acknowledged the independence of the church "in all matters spiritual" and the doctrine of two separate spheres of influence was reaffirmed.

ENGLAND

Since the Reformation the Crown has exercised considerable power in English ecclesiastical affairs. Under Henry VIII the Church of England could make a relatively smooth transition from Pope to King as supreme Head. This submission of church to state reached its ultimate in 1711 when the Convocation of Bishops and clergy was permitted to meet only once a year to pass an address of loyalty to the Crown. But it hasn't always been one-way traffic. In early Tudor times the Lords Spiritual had constituted half the membership of the Upper House. The Bishop of Durham was among the last personages to give up his private army. Today Bishops, Deans, and other senior clergy are state nominees, and no alteration of liturgy or doctrine is possible without the permission of Parliament. The Archbishops of Canterbury and York, the Bishops of London, Durham and Winchester together with another twenty-one senior diocesan bishops may sit in the Upper House. The 1968 proposals for reform of the House of Lords would reduce the number of bishops to sixteen. Contrary to popular opinion the Church in England receives no financial support from the state.

SCOTLAND TODAY

In the second half of the nineteenth century there were three major Presbyterian Churches in Scotland - the Established Church, the Free Church and the United Presbyterian Church. The last believed that the church should seek no support whatever from the civil government. The Free Church advocated national recognition and support of religion, provided that the liberty of the church was not compromised. In 1900 the United Presbyterian Church, which had existed since 1847, joined with the Free Church to form the United Free Church. After many complex goings on the Established Church and the United Free Church came together in the Union of 1929. Led by Principal Alexander Martin from the United Free Church side and Dr. John White of the Barony Church in Glasgow for the 'Auld Kirk' the last vestiges of state authority within the church were removed and a church was created which was both fully national and yet wholly free. The new relationship of the Church to the State was symbolised in the role of the Lord High Commissioner as representative of the Sovereign. This ancient office symbolises the national recognition of the church, but acknowledges that Christ alone is the Head of the Church. On this point Scotsmen have been as insistent as Englishmen have appeared indifferent. Today the Church of Scotland is the only Presbyterian Church in Britain which enjoys full national recognition. Because it has complete spiritual autonomy and is also the National Church of a nation that, at the moment, has no separate existence as a state its General Assembly not only prosecutes ecclesiastical business, but acts as a kind of National Forum. The debit side could well be that the radical emphasis of the United Free Church has been partly obscured in the rising climate of a self-conscious nationhood which has made the church increasingly nationalistic.

MODERN CATHOLICISM

What of the Roman Catholic Church today? Space prevents more than a brief note. In the latter part of the nineteenth century more and more Papal encyclicals were produced, followed later by interviews, press releases and radio messages from the Supreme Pontiff. This practice has grown, so that in 1952 alone Pius XII delivered over a dozen radio speeches, published 37 documents and directives,

16

and addressed numerous groups from cardinals to Rome telegraph boys. At the same time the Vatican Diplomatic Service has played an active but discreet role in international affairs. When the Vatican has felt that important moral issues were at stake as in debates on divorce and abortion the Catholic hierarchy has not been silent. But the contemporary world is not the Middle Ages and contemporary Catholic writers tend to stress the church as having power _in_ the world rather than _over_ the world. Such authority as she exercises in the political structures of society depends partly on her ability to be well-informed on complex issues and responsible in seeking for a fair solution of difficult problems. In Germany, Austria and Holland distinguished Catholic centres of research have been established. But her authority also depends on her ability to witness faithfully to the truth about human relationships as embodied in Christ's vision of the Kingdom of God on earth.

NON-EUROPEAN SOLUTIONS

Strict separation of church and state had been strongly advocated in the late seventeenth century by the philosopher John Locke. Under his influence the United States of America rejected any system in which the church was supported by the state. Canada followed suit as did Australia, which likewise rejected the English idea of an Establishment.

But the American separation is not as complete in fact as it sounds in theory. Congress is opened each day by prayer. Court oaths are taken on the Bible. Chaplains to the armed forces and government institutions are appointed and paid by the state.

To this day Protestant sects like the Mennonites have followed the Radical Reformers of the sixteenth century in refusing any kind of active participation in the political life of the country where they live. They believe that the church is a gathered fellowship of like-minded believers and in no sense a society which can be identified with a nation.

HOW TO GET INVOLVED

IN INTERNATIONAL AFFAIRS

Believing that the church should be more than a meeting place for
suburban households, Christians have sought for an effective way
to witness to Christ in the complex area of international affairs.
How does the gospel fit into the world of Oil Embargoes and
Strategic Arms Limitation? How can the church accept its due
responsibility for the right use of power without becoming a self-
appointed cabinet of amateur politicians?

SPECIALIST COMMITTEES

One of the most obvious attempts to answer this question has been
the setting up of specialist committees, usually on an ecumenical
basis, to guide the church on the complex political and economic
problems of the day. Two of the best known have been the
Commission of the Church on International Affairs, and the
Secretariat for Racial and Ethnic Relations. Both have done
valuable work in the World Council of Churches.

Similarly each denomination has its department which does
specialised study on international affairs. In the Church of
Scotland this task is undertaken by the Church and Nation Committee.

DO GOVERNMENTS LISTEN?

But there are many difficulties in this line of approach. In the
first place governments are not influenced much, if at all, by
high-sounding statements from bodies which have no direct electoral
significance. The more totalitarian a regime and the more blatant
its misuse of power the less likely is it that church statements
will be noted. One has only to consider Nazi Germany, White South
Africa, or Stalinist Russia to find that illustrated.

In the second place, the gospel itself gives no clear guidance
on the detailed technicalities associated with political decisions.
The Bible has nothing at all to say about the merits or demerits
of a United Europe, or about gold as the basis of an equitable
world monetary system. Surprisingly it gives very little clear
guidance on even broad moral issues like war or racism. Bible-in-
hand Christians have no miraculous recipe for the ills of the
world.

PRESSURE GROUPS

Most Christians who want to accept some measure of responsibility
for the ordering of international life feel dissatisfied with mere

church pronouncements. They want to make some contribution to building a fairer and better world. So they elect to join a pressure group and work with other like-minded people for a more just society. Organisations such as the Fellowship of Reconciliation and Amnesty International have had a strong appeal for some Christians. But church members who join do so as individuals. They do not commit the church as a whole.

And where the institution has taken a definite stand on controversial issues it has frequently seemed to lose its own distinctive voice and become comparable to any other pressure group. Opponents have contemptuously described it as "the Tribune with a halo" or "the Conservative Party at prayer". So Billy Graham's championing of President Nixon's hard-line on law and order appeared to many as the old temptation to give a religious dimension to a political stance. That is the inherent danger in the Christian political party. Such parties which have come into being largely in response to the challenge of secularism and communism have been active in West Germany, Italy, France, Belgium and the Netherlands. In Germany the Christian Democratic Union and in Italy the Christian Democratic Party have gradually moved from being left-wing and radical to being right-wing and conservative. More important neither party has given convincing evidence of being the standard-bearer of distinctively Christian policies.

It is, of course, right that Christians should join forces with men of goodwill who are seeking to bring about a just and peaceful society. It is natural that they should sometimes bind themselves together to struggle for what they believe to be right and true. It is true that from time to time they will inevitably be drawn into a costly confrontation with what is demonic and self-seeking in the world.

But how can the church engage in a genuinely creative struggle without seeming to become the self-appointed judge of the world? After all the New Testament says quite clearly that judgement is the prerogative of the Spirit (John 8: 50). Too often in the past when the church has appointed itself as the political and moral guardian of the world it has led to a peculiarly distasteful form of tyranny and authoriatarianism. The church is meant to be "a royal priesthood" (1 Peter 2: 9) not a shadow government offering an alternative policy to an evil world. And the unpalatable fact is that many of those who make no claim whatever to church allegiance have discerned far more clearly than the faithful the real moral issues and ethical dilemmas of political life.

The role of the church is not to offer alternative policies to those espoused by the party in power. It does not seek to gain power in the way that a shadow government hopes to be the next Cabinet. The church must give up the idea of a political power-base once and for all.

But if the church can have no political programme of its own and may not simply identify itself with the policy statements of another party what is left? What is its role?

THE ROLE OF THE CHURCH

The church exists to witness to a Person who was born in an out-house and died on a Roman gallows. It exercises that witness not by trying to remind society of what happened a long time ago in Palestine. Rather it bears witness to Jesus by embodying His Spirit in the world of today. It is called to be the place where Christ lives again in a word and action. As such it becomes the sign of the Kingdom, the embodiment of a new kind of society in which all men are seen as the recipients of a Father's unmerited love and the world as the one family of God. "There is one body, and one Spirit, one baptism, one God and Father of all" (Eph. 4: 4-6). And within the family diversity enriches rather than degrades. Mutual enrichment rather than exploitation is its purpose. "The eye cannot say to the hand: I do not need you. Quite the contrary: those organs of the body which seem to be more frail than others are indispensable" (1 Cor. 12: 21 f). Because the church is meant to be the visible sign of a Kingdom in which forgiveness, reconciliation, and active love are the only sure signs of God's Presence (Matt. 25: 31 f) it must seek to be present at the places in our society where division, hostility, injustice, illness, and sadness exist. The church is not a club in the world but a mission to the world. It does not exist for the sake of its members, but for the sake of embodying the love of Christ in the world of today.

A MINISTRY OF SUFFERING

When the church seeks to witness seriously in word and action to this kind of new community, when it responds to the call to be the visible sign of God's Kingdom on earth it encounters ridicule and opposition from those who are determined to enforce laws and attitudes which prevent a man from loving his brother. In a world where men prefer lies about other nations, races, classes, and each other, witnessing to the truth as exemplified in Christ will bring the cup of suffering.

HOW TO GET INVOLVED

IN LOCAL AFFAIRS

Whatever the difficulties facing an individual who wants to have
an influence in national and international politics there are
few who cannot play a valuable role locally.

VOLUNTARY ASSOCIATION

In every community there are specific problems affecting people.
Within a city these are often related to issues like homelessness,
decaying property in downtown areas, overcrowding in schools and
lack of adequate play facilities for children, the presence of
racial minorities and the siting of new roads and buildings which
affect long established residents. Individuals and voluntary
associations can do a great deal to help solve these problems and
smooth the inevitable upheavals associated with them.

KIRK SESSION AND CONGREGATION

The local congregation can have considerable influence in its
parish if it chooses to exercise it. Because it has no direct
political stake in the policies of the Right or Left it can act
as a genuine local forum for discussion, and point to the deeper
human issues involved. Informed prayer and relevant action
might seem much closer together if kirk sessions and congregations
were to invite those who work in the decision-making machinery of
local government to share their concerns at a Sunday service.

One of the most notable examples of this in history was the
Clapham Sect, a group of evangelical English laymen of the
eighteenth century committed to make the faith relevant to
ordinary life. They shared prayers and Bible Study, and then
went out to deal with social issues like slavery. Aims were dis-
cussed, hopes shared, and work delegated. It was an immensely
effective organisation and showed just how much can be achieved
when Christians come together in fellowship and service. It also
showed that Christians can only make a useful contribution when
they take the trouble to understand the problems thoroughly, and
have grasped the range of options which are open.

A modern writer tells how a Protestant minister and a
Catholic priest brought together in 1960 in Chicago 13 churches
and over 75 other groups to deal with a slum area. The organisation was successful in getting the negroes of the area to do
something for themselves, in forcing bad landlords to improve
their property, and in achieving a new sense of status and well-
being for the whole community. In the U.K. the problems might

well be different, but many a church would make an immediate impact if it examined some similar kind of strategy for its own mission to the community.

POSITIONS OF LEADERSHIP

Christians can themselves seek positions of responsibility where they can shape the life of the community for the common good. But they do so not from any motives of personal aggrandisement, but as concerned members of the Christian Church.

Contrary to popular conceptions local politics offer very few laurels to the office-holder. Much of the work is slow, routine and unappreciated. The peace of anonymity has to be sacrificed for duties which are time-consuming and seldom offer any kind of financial gain. The Christian in government will find his motives suspect, his decisions misrepresented, and his failures remembered. Occasionally he may have to compromise in situations where half a loaf is better than no bread at all and few solutions are ideal on all accounts.

Politics is never a simple matter of good and bad, but of balancing many different priorities. Little causes may have to be sacrificed to greater ones, relationships nurtured or played down, and individual preferences subordinated to an overall plan.

There will be plenty of disappointment and stress. It is a fortunate councillor who can draw on the prayers and appreciation of a Christian congregation, even though some members may question whether his own remedies for civic problems are the best ones.

PARTY MEMBER AND VOTER

Most obvious of all the Christian can be politically well-informed and where temperament and time permit an active member of a political party. As a voter he can play a small part in determining which candidate will represent his community. But as a party member he can help decide what the priorities of the party platform shall be. Not every one can hope to be at the centre of the decision-making process. But each individual who is willing to take some time and trouble can find opportunities to contribute to his party's thinking. At a time when local politics are beset with a pervasive air of boredom and partisanship, Christians willing to take a real interest in local affairs can make a quite vital contribution to the health of the community debate and political decision-making.

Since the end of the Second World War people living in both America and Europe have become used to seeing demonstrations as a means of registering protest. In this country we have witnessed the Campaign for Nuclear Disarmament, the Stop the Seventy Springbok Tour, the Festival of Light Rallies, and various political demonstrations all directed to bringing about specific change. In the United States the Civil Rights Movement and the Peace in Vietnam demonstrations attracted a lot of support.

This type of demonstration is not new. In the earlier part of the century direct action was used to effect by the suffragettes, the unemployed from Jarrow and South Wales, and Sir Oswald Mosley's Union of Fascists. But as a pattern of behaviour mass demonstrations seem to be on the increase. They raise acute ethical problems for the Christian, especially when voilence seems likely to ensue.

On the one hand it is clear that the most obdurate structures of injustice are often not sufficiently amenable to reasons and moral appeal. Hitler's Germany and Stalin's Russia witness to that. So direct action may be the only answer. As Rudi-Weber has put it: "The mission of peace is a struggle which may cost more than our peace of mind or promotion - it may cost our life." Violence has achieved very real changes in some societies.

On the other hand it is clear that in His relationships with people Jesus remained absolutely loyal to the principle of love instead of force. Similarly the earliest Christians repudiated violence and coercion as an instrument of social change.

In 1969 and 1973 large numbers of Christians throughout the United Kingdom appended their names to a Declaration on World Poverty which urged the government to give due consideration to the needs of the Third World. Such a petition is not without value as an expression of public opinion. But in the end the Christian is aware that some kind of sacrificial action is required of him as well as a declaration of concern. When all lawful means of protest have been exhausted to little or no effect some type of direct civil disobedience may remain the only alternative.

THE PARTY SYSTEM

THE CONSERVATIVE PARTY

The Conservatives, one of the two major political parties in
Britain, are the successors of the old Tory Party. Opponents
often use the older word because the term "tory" was first applied
to Irish bandits.

Shortly after the Reform Bill of 1832 the new "conservative"
party emerged, as Disraeli later put it, "to maintain the institutions of the country, uphold the Empire, and ameliorate the
condition of the people". This stress on maintaining a tradition
is basic to the conservative creed. As recently as 1957 Harold
MacMillan on his appointment as Party Leader used Disraeli's phrase
to describe the party's standpoint: "We must be conservative to
conserve all that is good and radical to uproot all that is bad".
The right wing in British politics has continuously been represen-
ted by the Conservative Party for nearly 150 years.

Originally the party supported the landed interests, the
prerogatives of the crown, and the power of the Church of England.
With the growth of imperialism the building up and extension of
the British Empire became an important part of its policy. Since
the First World War it has championed as much of the retention of
British power overseas as possible, and upheld the right of private
ownership and the free competitive society as opposed to socialism
and state planning.

Between the two World Wars the Conservatives, whose fortunes
had sunk to a low ebb during the period 1902-14, were almost continuously in power either alone or as a coalition. During Hitler's
war Churchill led a coalition but the success of his war effort
was personal rather than political. In the election of 1945 the
Conservatives were heavily defeated.

For the next six years the party reviewed its whole policy
under the dynamic chairmanship of Lord Woolton, and published
important documents like "The Industrial Charter" which sought
to re-think old principles in the light of new situations. In
particular it visualised an economic and social system in which
employers and employees, private enterprise and the state would
co-operate to their mutual advantage.

In 1951 the Conservative Party was returned to power. It
remained in office until 1964 under four successive Prime
Ministers; Churchill, Eden, MacMillan and Douglas-Home, and
increased its majority in 1955 and 1959.

During this period the Welfare State established by its pre-
decessors was consolidated, many former colonies were granted

24

dominion status and others prepared for self-government, and a determined though unsuccessful attempt was made to enter the Common Market.

However, it was not all plain sailing. The party was severely rocked by two crises, namely the military intervention in Egypt at the Suez Canal in 1956 and the sensational Profumo affair in 1963. The following year Mr. Edward Heath was elected as leader by the Conservative Parliamentary Party. The pace of African independence and the gradual acceptance of a mixed economy helped to give rise to a more right wing group within the party with dissident views on defence, immigration, and taxation. This movement, though comparatively small in numbers among Parliamentarians, has a broader base in the local constituencies. It finds its voice in politicians like Enoch Powell, M.P. for South Down, and its nurture in the so-called Monday Club.

While opposed to state ownership, the modern Conservative Party has tended to accept the nationalisation acts of its Labour opponents with the exception of road transport and steel. Its general economic policy continues to emphasize the value of free enterprise though in practice it recognises that this must operate within the framework of much state planning. On social and Commonwealth policies it differs from its political opponents only in terms of emphasis and priority.

After six years in opposition the party was returned to power in June 1970. It was the beginning of a term of office which was to witness a dramatic shift in the political fortunes and economic power of the Arab bloc at the expense of the major European industrial nations. Faced with huge increases in oil costs and spiralling inflation, especially in food and housing, Mr. Heath introduced the Industrial Relations Bill. It led to bitter conflict between the government and the unions which culminated in the three-day working week and the miners' strike. In February 1974 Mr. Heath sought a clear mandate from the electorate but failed to get it. After abortive moves for a coalition with the Liberals had broken down, the Conservatives returned to the opposition benches.

When the hustings resumed seven months later, the Conservatives campaigned on the theme of a Party of National Unity and commitment to Europe. Given the failure to win earlier in the year the party did better than could reasonably have been expected. In particular it prevented Labour from turning a small advantage into a large majority as it had done in 1966. But to limit loss is not to win victory and many commentators felt that for all his courage and ability Mr. Heath lacked the warmth of popular appeal. Perhaps the memories of the previous winter's confrontation were too fresh to convince the electorate that he could heal the wounds of a divided and anxious nation.

In the Spring of 1975 the party made political history by electing Mrs. Margaret Thatcher as its leader in place of Edward Heath.

THE LABOUR PARTY

The Labour Party, the other major force in British politics today, dates back as a parliamentary force to the 1906 election when it secured 29 seats in the Commons. It grew out of a nucleus of trade unions, co-operative societies and other smaller socialist bodies which banded together to secure political representation. Its pragmatic Trade Union roots and the tradition of intellectual Christian Socialism ensured that the British Labour Movement never became anti-clerical as it tended to do in predominantly catholic countries.

It strongly supported the war effort against the Kaiser's Germany and its leader at that time, Arthur Henderson, was included in the coalition.

After the Armistice the Labour Party withdrew its support from the government and adopted a new socialist constitution for the first time with the stated aim of securing "the common owner-ship of the means of production". Local branches of the party were set up and individual members were admitted. This was an important step for it gave the right to the local constituency party to appoint the agent, confirm the selection of individuals to fight local elections, nominate the parliamentary candidate and designate delegates to the Annual Conference.

Membership rose steeply and by 1922 the Labour Party was recognised as the official opposition. In 1924 it formed a minority government for a few months under Ramsay MacDonald with Liberal support.

In the elections of May 1929 the Labour Party gained a majority over the Conservatives for the first time, but less than two years later the government resigned in the face of the severe economic crisis and was replaced by a coalition. A real parli-amentary breakthrough came in the 1945 election when the party won 393 seats and took office for the first time as a majority govern-ment. Mr. Clement Attlee became the Prime Minister.

The new government pursued a policy of developing the Welfare State. Essential services and industries such as the coal mines, electricity, gas, railways, and the Bank of England were national-ised. A fully comprehensive system of national insurance was instituted (1946) as was a National Health Service (1948). Though the attempt to create a moderate socialist state largely succeeded, the Labour government did not cope altogether successfully with the economic problems of the post-war era. In 1951 the Conservatives again gained power.

For the next 13 years the Labour Party devoted much of its energy to a bitter internal dispute. The followers of Aneurin Bevan wanted a purer form of socialism with increased nationalisation and further disarmament. But others believed that Labour's apparent commitment to the more extreme policies of the Left was responsible for its continued poor showing at the polls.

The 1964 election narrow win for Labour led by the new leader, Mr. Harold Wilson, was consolidated in March 1966 when the government was returned with a majority of 97. In spite of serious economic problems, culminating in the devaluation of the pound and large local by-election losses, the public opinion polls indicated that the Labour Party would win the 1970 election. It failed by 30 seats. Recent political commentators have detected a new left-wing militancy which has had a perceptible influence on the policy statements of the party.

After further elections in February 1974, the Queen invited Mr. Wilson to form a minority government. Later that same year his Labour administration, campaigning on a manifesto in which a social contract with the trade unions was the cornerstone, secured the support of about 40 per cent of the electorate and a tiny overall parliamentary majority of three. Mr. Wilson's adroitness in surviving with narrow margins is widely acknowledged. His first call for a spirit of national unity - ironically the main theme of the Conservative platform - suggested that the expectations of the more extreme left-wing of the party were unlikely to be fulfilled in the immediate future. Led by Mr. Wedgwood Benn it campaigned vigorously for British disengagement from the European Economic Community. In a National Referendum on 5th June, 1975, the people overwhelmingly reaffirmed Britain's ties with Europe.

THE LIBERAL PARTY

In the late eighteenth century Members of Parliament tended to collect into small pressure groups. Most were either Whig or Tory. Broadly speaking the Tory emphasized the old rule of privilege and the Crown while the Whig was the democrat.

The supporters of the Presbyterian cause in Scotland were also called Whigs, and the Liberals were their indirect heirs following the Reform Bill of 1832. They backed the transfer of control from the aristocrats to the more radical industrialists, and drew most of their support from nonconformists and the middle class. Indeed the distinction between the Free Churches and the Church of England was one of the most important and lasting guides to political allegiances between Liberal and Conservative.

Central to all Liberal ideals is a belief in the value of the individual. From this have come many traits of the Liberal Party, notably its trust in rationality, its faith in the idea of progress, its attachment to individualism, its emphasis on human rights and its eagerness to emancipate underprivileged groups. As such it has always claimed to be the genuine left wing of British politics. But its distrust of the functions of the state has sometimes impelled it towards the right.

At home, Liberal reforms have moulded most of Britain's political institutions. Abroad, its policies have been generally internationalist and often pacifist with a marked antipathy to imperialism.

During their first period in government (1830-41) the Liberal Party promoted parliamentary reform and the abolition of slavery. But its utilitarian and laissez-faire theories led to the harsh Poor Law of 1834. Later the Party's left wing, composed mostly of working-class radicals, repudiated the laissez-faire ideology and inclined towards republicanism.

In the latter part of the nineteenth century the Liberals drew on the inspiration and leadership of many notable names including Bentham, Bright, Cobden, J. S. Mill, Lord Palmerston and W. E. Gladstone, the latter being Prime Minister on no fewer than four occasions. Throughout this period most of Scotland and Wales was predominantly Liberal as were the industrial areas of the Midlands and North East England.

Under Gladstone's banner of "Peace, Retrenchment and Reform" the Victorian Liberals championed free trade and the establishment of civil and political liberty. Universal male suffrage was achieved in 1884, and other important reforms introduced included elementary education and vote by ballot.

When the party split over Home Rule in 1886 many joined the Conservatives, and the Liberals exercised little direct political power until 1905. Many Liberals believed that with a minimum of state interference and government in the hands of the people instead of a single class individual enterprise and energy would of itself bring well-being to the whole community. It soon became apparent that this was too simple a view. The community acting through the State must be responsible for providing educational facilities and safeguards against poverty and insecurity.

During the first part of the twentieth century the Liberal governments of Bannerman and Asquith placed a great deal of social legislation on the statute book. It included old age pensions, national insurance, the limitation of the powers of the Lords, and the Irish Home Rule Bill. The Housing and Town Planning Act was a first step toward the abolition of slums. Prior to 1914 the Liberals' main policy programme rested on four main pillars - Land Reform, Home Rule, Free Trade and Temperance Reform.

The failure of the party to attract the newly-enfranchised working class after the First World War and the rise of the Labour movement both contributed to the gradual decline of the Liberals. Leaders included Asquith, Lloyd George and Churchill.

The Liberals joined the National Government in 1931 but broke away in protest against a protectionist policy. Since then they have never held office, but their political influence has far exceeded their number of parliamentary seats.

The Liberal Party was the first political party to advocate family allowances and support the important Beveridge Report of 1942 on which subsequent social security legislation in the U.K. was largely based. The party urged Britain's entry into the European Economic Community long before the Conservatives attempted to secure it. Today it espouses the idea of separate parliaments for Scotland and Wales.

Debate has centred on its ability to break the long-established two party system and act as a moderate centre party free from union domination from the left and business interests on the right. The signs of a major Liberal revival in the winter election of 1974 were not fully realised in the autumn election of that same year.

Though the party fielded over 600 candidates, openly advocated a statutory freeze on wages and prices, and secured almost 20 per cent of the total votes cast, it had to be content with just thirteen seats in the new House of Commons.

THE SCOTTISH NATIONAL PARTY

The Scottish National Party came into being in 1934 as a result of the merger of two other nationalist movements, the National Party of Scotland and the Scottish Party. Its policy has centred on self-government but with joint responsibility with England for defence, foreign policy and customs tariffs.

In 1942 the moderate Home Rulers left the party and launched a National Assembly and Covenant. Six years later all those who were members of other parties were expelled and the nucleus continued as a small relatively unnoticed group. By 1962 its membership was down to a mere 2,000.

The Party's fortunes have varied. In 1945 R. D. McIntyre won a by-election in Motherwell and took his seat as the Party's first representative in the Commons. He lost it three months later in the General Election.

In 1967 another S.N.P. candidate, Mrs. Winifred Ewing, took the safe Labour seat of Hamilton. At the Party Conference in 1969 the delegates failed to agree on a detailed policy statement but looked with satisfaction on a membership of around 100,000 organised in 500 branches.

In the early 1970s the discovery of substantial deposits of oil in the North Sea, a growing disillusionment with membership of the European Economic Community, and a widespread feeling that Scotland had been getting a poor deal for too long combined to create a new mood of optimism and national self-awareness north of the border. This resulted in a greatly increased support for the Nationalist cause. Notable electoral advance in the February 1974 election when seven candidates were successful was a warning shot to the other major parties that the S.N.P. was about to establish itself as a significant political force in British politics. When it secured another four seats at the October election and out-polled the Conservatives to win full 30 per cent of the popular vote it was clear that Scottish Nationalism could no longer be treated with Westminster's customary polite disinterest.

What of the future? Are we witnessing the birth of a new political galaxy, or merely one of those sudden upsurges of fortune which the nationalist cause has known before and which disappears as speedily as a meteor in the night? Its leaders hope for the former. But seasoned politicians are all too aware that it is a big task to transform a widespread mood into a settled political commitment. The outcome may well be affected as much by the level of employment, the Common Market Referendum, and the powers of a separate Scottish Assembly as by arguments on the merits or demerits of a fully independent Scotland within a United Kingdom modelled on the Scandinavian pattern.

As devolutionists and long-standing supporters of an independent Parliament for Scotland the Liberals briefly toyed with the idea of an electoral agreement between the two parties. Such an alliance would have provided an invaluable source of proven leadership and competency to the S.N.P. movement. Though it never materialised many influential voices within the country and all official party manifestoes now support some kind of national Assembly in Scotland to deal with internal issues.

THE COMPOSITION OF THE MAIN PARTIES

Differences in the social background of the parties in the Commons have become less marked since the Second World War. The Conservative is still largely the Party of the Establishment, with the aristocracy and upper middle class coming from English public schools dominant. Its parliamentary party consists largely of company directors, lawyers, farmers and landowners, journalists and publishers.

In contrast, Labour M.P.s include many of working class origin.

Grammar school rather than public school accents tend to predominate. An increasing number of members including trade union officials now tend to have some form of higher education. In recent years, while manual workers have significantly been less in evidence, the leadership has had a markedly impressive intellectual strength and this has probably helped to attract middle class support.

The small number of Liberal M.P.s makes any kind of generalisation open to question. Its image is predominantly middle class with traditional support tending to come from agricultural areas like the Borders and the island constituencies in Northern Scotland.

ARE PARTY POLITICS INEVITABLE?

Party politics have been criticised for centuries. To speak of "toeing the party line" is regarded as derogatory, and the ordinary voter is suspicious of politicians generally. In part this may be due to the common practice among candidates of all persuasion of securing electoral support by promising more than can be ultimately given. Once in power most governments find the room for manoeuvre strictly curtailed by economic and social considerations which they may influence but seldom control.

Nevertheless it seems probable that most of the electorate expect a clear and simple statement of policy from a party before voting in its favour. It is equally true that political life in this country is remarkably free of graft and corruption. For the most part those elected work hard, put in long hours of service for which they receive only a modest income of £4,500 per annum and are frequently well informed on a wide range of issues.

APPENDIX

Scripture   Exodus 4-5
Passages   Amos 5: 13-16
for Study: Jeremiah 22: 13-16
            Matthew 25: 31-46
            Romans 13
            1 Peter 2: 11-25
            Revelation 13

Books   *William Wilberforce* by Oliver Warner (Batsford)
for Study: *Elizabeth Fry* by John Whitney (Harrap)
            Trevor Huddleston (People with a purpose series) by
                Ian Birnie (SCM)
            Dietrich Bonhoeffer by E. Bethge (Collins)
            Martin Luther King by Coretta Scott King (Hodder)
            George MacLeod (People with a purpose series) by
                Sheila Hobden (SCM)

Quotable   Christianity has nothing to do with "the cause of
Quotes: trendy fashion, aid, race concern, pollution and the
            rest. The social gospel warning us not to be indif-
            ferent to those who need our help has dissolved."
            (Enoch Powell, M.P., writing in <u>The Times</u>)

"To say that religion has nothing to do with a man's
attitude to the system in which he lives and indeed
for which he legislates - nothing to do with any moral
duties or obligations - in other words nothing to do
with the actions of his daily political life is surely
not only distorted but immoral as well."
(Nadir Dinshaw in <u>New Outlook</u>, 1972-3)

"If politics is an art, it is one of the performing
arts, and not one of the creative ones."
(From <u>Ethics and Politics</u> by Maurice Cranston in
   <u>Encounter</u>, June 1972)

"To educate the young people into religious ways may
perhaps be the task of the church, but to educate
the young in politics is very much our affair .....
For the churches there is only one solution, which
will ensure peace: back into the sacristy. Let the

churches serve God; we serve the people."
(<u>Volkischer Beobachter</u>, Aug. 1935 - a weekly gossip
  which Hitler took over as his personal newspaper)

"Politics do not belong in the church."
(Slogan of the German National Socialist Party, quoted
  in <u>The Nazi Persecution of the Churches</u> by J. S.
  Conway)

"Let the church discover and identify itself with
groups of people that suffer because of unjust situations, and who have no way of making themselves heard.
The church should be the voice of those who have no
one. The church must discover those groups and
identify herself with them. Here is the modern Way
of the Cross, the way of Christian responsibility."
(Emilio Castro, quoted in <u>The Development Apocalypse</u>)

"Every Catholic who is not a revolutionary and is not
on the side of the revolutionaries lives in mortal
sin."
(Father Camilo Torres - a Roman Catholic priest who
  joined the Bolivian guerrilla movement and was
  killed in a clash with the security forces)

"It is a question, rather, of building a world where
every man no matter what his race, religion, or
nationality can live a fully human life, freed from
servitude imposed on him by other men or by natural
forces over which he has not sufficient control; a
world where freedom is not an empty word and where
the poor man Lazarus can sit down at the same table
with the rich man."
(<u>Progressio populorum</u> - official Statement from the
  bishops of Latin America)

"God comes to us today in the events of social change,
in what theologians have often called history, what
we call politics. But events of social change need
not mean upheavals and revolutions. The events of
everyday life are also events of social change."
(Harvey Cox in <u>The Secular City</u>)

"Right politics is religion."
(J. A. T. Robinson in <u>On Being the Church in the
  World</u>)

"The church's role is to give a moral lead, not in
episcopal utterances or synodical statements alone
but by the determined efforts of all its ordinary
members where they are. It is the Christian community of this country which should, by protest, by
vote and - where necessary - by direct action make
clear its concern for the hungry world and for
justice in race relations everywhere."
(Father Trevor Huddleston in a letter to The Times)

"To be gentle and humble ... is not the same thing as
being weak and easy-going."
(Pope John XXIII)

"Strange isn't it how many people there are who
would rather go to church than be the church."
(A Parishioner's jottings)

Points for
Research
and
Discussion:

1. Can you find out what is the political meaning
   of the terms "left wing" and "right wing"?

2. Who were the Tolpuddle Martyrs, what did they
   accomplish, and have they any lessons to teach
   us today?

3. How far should a government's control of
   society extend?

4. Do you think it is better to be dead than Red?

5. What do Christian people mean when they speak
   of "hope"?

6. Find out all you can about the political and
   civic life of your home town or area. In
   particular:

   a) How many people voted in the last local
      election?

   b) Who is your local councillor?

   c) What are the most important social problems
      facing your community?

   d) What is the party in power doing about each
      of them?

   e) How often are meetings of the Council held
      and where can the Minutes be read?

   f) What are the local political parties concerned
      about and how can a more interested audience
      be built up?

g) Can you discover one area of social work which is in need of voluntary helpers?

h) How could you best help meet that need?

For Further Reading:

Cry the Beloved Country by Alan Paton (Cape, 1948)

Tomorrow's Sun by Helen Joseph (Hutchinson, 1968)

Race against Time by Helder Camara (Sheed & Ward, 1971)

On Being the Church in the World by J. A. T. Robinson (SCM, 1960)

Calvary Now by Ambrose Reeves (SCM, 1965)

On Not Leaving it to the Snake by Harvey Cox (SCM, 1968)

The Secular City by Harvey Cox (Billing & Sons, 1967)

Law, Love and Language by Herbert McCabe (Sheed & Ward, 1968)   (Also available in paperback)

The Political Christ by Alan Richardson (SCM, 1973)

A Theology for Radical Politics by Michael Novak (Herder and Herder, 1969)

The Political Background of the New Testament by Stewart Perowne (Hodder and Stoughton, 1965)

****